To..................................

From............................

Collect all 28 of
Purple Ronnie's Little Books

Little Guide to Boyfriends
Little Poems for Friends
Little Guide for Lovers
Little Book of Willies and Bottoms
Little Guide to Men
Little Guide to Girls
Little Book of Pants
Little Guide to Doing It
Little Guide to Life
Little Book of Love Poems
Little Book of Football
Little Thoughts about Mums
Little Thoughts about Dads
Little Poems to say I Love You
Little Kama Sutra
Little Guide to Your New Baby
Little Guide to Getting Married
Little Book of Chocolate
Little Thoughts about Christmas
Little Book of Love
Little Book for a Lovely Mum
Little Book for a Smashing Dad
Little Book for a Lovely Grandma
Little Book for a Smashing Grandad
Little Book for The World's Best Boyfriend
Little Book for The World's Best Girlfriend
Little Book for The World's Best Mum
Little Book for The World's Best Dad

... and all 12 of Purple Ronnie's
Little Star Signs

...and Purple Ronnie's Bloke's
Guide to Life, the Universe
and Bottom Burps

Purple Ronnie's
Ultimate
Toilet Book

The Funniest Book for the Smallest Room in the House

hee hee

FOOTIE CARS GIRLS BEER

by Purple Ronnie

First published 2009 by Boxtree
an imprint of Pan Macmillan Ltd
Pan Macmillan, 20 New Wharf Road, London N1 9RR
Basingstoke and Oxford
Associated companies throughout the world
www.panmacmillan.com

ISBN 978-0-7522-2701-6

Some of the material in this book was previously published under the titles
Purple Ronnie's Guide to Life, The Smashing World of Purple Ronnie, Purple Ronnie's Star Signs,
Purple Ronnie's Guide to Men and Purple Ronnie's Guide to Girls,

'Purple Ronnie' created by Giles Andreae. The right of Giles Andreae and Janet Cronin
to be identified respectively as the author and illustrator of this work has been asserted by them
in accordance with the Copyright, Designs and Patents Act 1988.

1 3 5 7 9 8 6 4 2

A CIP catalogue record for this book is available from
the British Library.

Printed and bound in Great Britain by Butler Tanner & Dennis Ltd, Frome

Visit www.panmacmillan.com to read more about all our books
and to buy them. You will also find features, author interviews and
news of any author events, and you can sign up for e-newsletters
so that you're always first to hear about our new releases.

a poem about
↓
The Lav

Of all the most fabulous
      things I can do
And the smashingest times
           I can have
There isn't a pleasure I love
           quite as much
As settling down on the Lav

Contents

Men Types

a poem about
Macho Men

Some men think it's cool to bare
A bulging chest with loads of hair
But if you talk to one you'll find
His brains are stuck up his behind

a poem about
Girly Men

Girly Men think playing sport is too rough
So they love to go shopping instead
And when they get home
They spend hours on the phone
Before wearing their face masks to bed

a poem about
Lager Lads

Lager Lads love going out with their mates

In fact it's their favourite trick

To gobble down masses of curry and beer

And pass out in piles of sick

a poem about a
Sport Man

No girl can get close to a Sport Man
Without passing out on the spot
The air in his room
Has the subtle perfume
Of the sweat on a wrestler's bot

a poem about ↓

Weeds

Some Men think weeds are pathetic
Because they're so fussy and neat
But most people find
That they're friendly and kind
And girls always say that they're sweet

a poem about Slobs

They walk around in clouds of smoke
They splutter burp and wheeze
They live off mouldy sausages
And whiff of rancid cheese

Wide Boys

They're always on their mobile phones
cutting dodgy deals
Looking sharp in shiny suits
And nifty sets of wheels

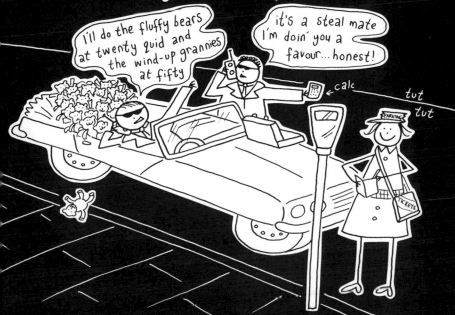

a poem about a
Perfect Man

Most girls want a man who is perfect
But maybe not many exist
Who've got charm and panache
Several sackloads of cash
And a willy the size of your wrist

Warning :-
Ladettes like to tell you all about every other person they've slept with

Special Tip:-

Ladettes always love Doing It in interesting places

Mumsy Girls love
to spank naughty
little boys

Warning:-

Mumsy Girls love Doing It so they can make babies

Posh Girls are not afraid to tell you what to do in bed and they are often quite demanding

Warning:-
Posh Girls can sometimes
have some rather
strange fantasies

Warning:-

Girly Girls don't really like Doing It. They think it's all a bit messy

Girly Girls are amazing
flirts and they know
exactly how to get
any man they want

Special Tip

Nothing turns an Earth Mother on more than a good sniff of your armpits

Earth Mothers make great lovers because they are so in touch with their bodies

Hippy Chicks

The Moon always
makes Hippy Chicks
feel incredibly sexy

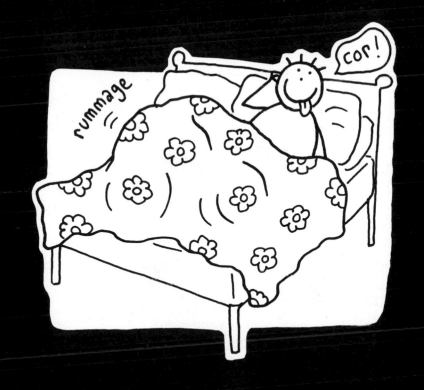

When they're in the mood
Hippy Chicks are brilliant at
Doing it and they love trying
out all sorts of new tricks

Special Tip:-
It is best not to let a
Sporty Girl see you
naked until she is
completely in love with you

Sporty Girls are so fit that it usually only takes one drink to get them completely pissed

Lots of men are too
frightened to date Sex
Goddesses so they often
end up with the kind of
boyfriends you might not expect

Warning :-

When you are Doing It
with a Sex Goddess
it is best to think of
something completely different
if you want it to last for more
than 5 seconds

warm and
cuddly
Love Snuggle

<u>S</u>pecial Tip:-

Perfect Girls make
you feel like this
feeling's never
going to end

When a Perfect Girl kisses you for the first time your whole body wants to explode with happiness

a poem about a
↓
Sexy Girl

There's loads of tempting thingies
That can make a bloke's head
swirl
But the best of these
Has got to be
A gorgeous sexy girl !

constellation
under-pantus →

Star
Signs

⭐ Special Tip. ⭐

If you want to Do It with an Aquarian you must tell them it's their brains you fancy them for

an Aquarian is never normal

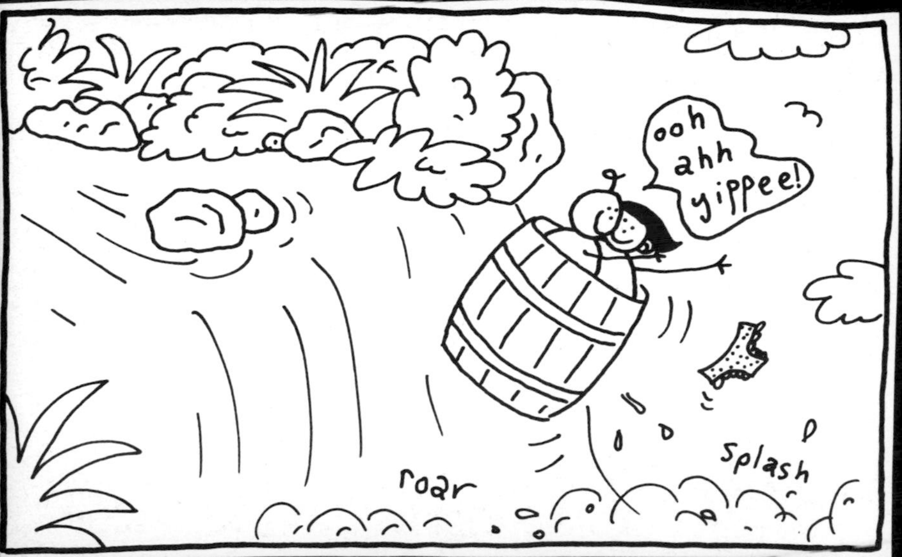

Pisceans are not
sex-mad and
they only like
Doing It with people
who they love

☆ Special Tip ☆

A Pisces always loves Doing It underwater

Ariens are completely sex-mad.
They love Doing It in all sorts of
places at any time of the day

Arien women love being on
top and most of them
eat men for breakfast

Taurus

A Taurus in love is unlikely ever to Do It with someone else but they can get incredibly jealous of their partners

Taureans are brilliant at planning special nights of LOVE

smelly candles

wiggle

masses of love cake

Geminis like their sex life to be fun and playful and full of surprises

Geminis never stop talking even when they're Doing It

Cancer

Most Cancer people are brilliant in bed and like to learn all about your favourite Love Tricks

Cancer

Cancers are worried about catching diseases so they always wear lots of protection

When it comes to Doing It Leos always like to be in charge

☆ **Special Tip** ☆

A Leo who wants
you for sex will want
you for love and
friendship as well

Virgos can go for ages without having sex but once they find someone they fancy, they want to Do It with them till their bits drop off

☆ Special Tip ☆

Most of all Virgos like
Doing It in the shower
because it's clean and tidy
and doesn't mess up the bed

when a Libran
wants to Do It with
you they like to make
sure it's the best sex
you've ever had

☆_Special Tip_☆

Some Librans
prefer reading about
sex to actually
Doing It

Scorpios love flirting and talking about all sorts of rude things

Scorpios are crazy
about rude sex because
it lets out all their
bottled up feelings

When it comes to Doing It Sagittarians love to experiment and try out all sorts of new things

Sagittarians always feel sexy in aeroplanes

a poem about
↓

Best Signs

Virgo, Libra, Cancer, Aries

Yes, and all the rest

Of all the Star Signs

Girls can be

Which do you like best?

Pants

man
thong

Purple Ronnie's Guide to PANTS

Pant Fact 1

Pants were the first invention ever in the whole world. The first pants were made of leaves and bits of string

G-String Pants

G-String Pants are like tying
a tiny hanky round your parts.
Do not wear G-string pants
if you have a flabby bottom
Cos you might not find them
again for ages

String Pants

No-one knows why string
pants were invented. Do not
wear them infront of girls.
String pants are good for
straining homemade beer and
catching fish

French Pants

sexy silk undies →

French pants are for looking sexy in. They are so slippery that if you aren't careful you can slide off your chair and collapse on the floor

not sexy →

skid

Squashing Pants

Squashing pants squish your tummy and bottom together to make you look thinner when you wear squashing pants steam comes out of your ears, you walk in a funny way and sometimes bits of tummy squish out over the edge

Granny Pants

Granny Pants stretch from just under your armpits to just above your feet. They are made from thick baggy sacks and are covered in frills. Granny pants always smell of poison

Sports Pants

Sports pants are for squeezing men's bits into the smallest shape possible. Only to be worn for short periods of time or your privates might melt

How to...

1. How to keep your Relationship Healthy with Your Girlfriend:

Tell her that she's special,

The only one for you,

Find out what she really likes

And make her murmur, "OOoooh!"

you

v. happy girlfriend

rummage

2. How to Give the Gift of Flowers:

A bunch of flowers works magic

Most girls like flowers
it's true

But don't forget to add some words

like "Munchkin, I Love YOU!"

3. How to Break up Peacefully:

Don't tell a girl she's
                    boring
When love and romance
                    ends
Cos it's better to be kinder
And end up being friends

4. How to ask Someone On a Date:

Don't seem mad or desperate
When asking for a date
And don't turn up too early
But <u>never</u> be too late!

5. How to Compliment A Woman who Catches Your Eye:

When women go out looking gorgeous
They know they can really excite
It's great if you tell them how lovely they look
But make sure you keep it polite

6. How to Write a Love Letter:

If you've fallen in love with a lady
And your feelings are starting to fizz
Write them a long soppy letter
Cos they know how lovely LOVE is

ooh he's so _so_ amazing!

brilliant love letter

7. How to Win With Hair Loss:

Comb-overs, lotions, and
anti-bald potions
Are useless, so don't even
try
Wear it shaven or short
Like an older guy ought
And you might still just catch
a girl's eye!

8. How to Use Your Moustache :

I've heard a neatly trimmed
moustache

Can really be a thriller
So keep it clean and tidy
And you'll be a lady killer!

9. <u>How to Throw a Party</u>:

A party needs some funky sounds
That make you want to bop
So ask round all your bestest mates
And boogie til you drop!

10. How to Avoid a Hangover:

To keep away a hangover
Before you go to bed
Drink masses of cold water
To try and clear your head
But here's an extra little tip
That really can't be missed -
When you go out drinking
Don't get so bloomin' pissed!

11. How to Start a Fan Club:

A fan club needs a person
To worship or adore
It helps if they are talented
Or beautiful or more
But I wonder what would
                    happen...
Well, let's just wait and see
If someone tried to start a
                    fan club
Simply about <u>ME</u>!

Beer

a poem about
↓

DRINKING BEER

If you're down the pub these
days
You're not allowed to smoke
Which makes things rather tricky
For a certain sort of bloke
So why do men still got there?
Well, the answers pretty clear —
A whole great bloomin' cellarful
Of lovely LOVELY beer!

a poem about

BREWING BEER

You know when you're making
your homebrew
That the skills have been
thoroughly mastered
When all of your mates drink
so much of the stuff
That they all end up totally
plastered!

a poem about
↓
THE PUB

When you're down in the dumps
and the doldrums

And life seems depressing and
drear

Drop into the pub
Get a plate of good grub
And a glass of delicious cool
beer!

a poem about
↓
A L E

Warm ale that comes out of
                    barrels
Is what real blokes like best
But sometimes they end up
Just looking as if
There's a barrel right under
                    their vest

a poem about
↓

BEER TYPES

Lager, bitter, brown ale, stout,
Too much makes you sway
and shout

But just enough makes
headaches clear

And fills you up with
friendly cheer!

hooray!

← happy
beer
glow

a poem about
↓
BEER and STYLE

Some blokes drink their
beer with poise
And treat it like an art
But some just glug it greedily
And slurp and belch and fart!

a poem about ↓

THE BEER DRINKER'S PRAYER

I pray that I'm not alcoholic

That would be too great a test

I might have to give up my favourite beers

And beer is the stuff I like best!

a poem about ↓

BEER and YOUR WILLY

Beer makes blokes get
 frisky
But they end up feeling silly
Cos they really want to DO IT
But they can't control their
 willy!

a poem about
TYPES OF BEER

Some guys like a real ale, that's
          brown and thick and hearty
Some guys hold a bottle looking
          casual at a party
Some guys think a six-pack
          makes them seem a real man
But some guys aren't so choosey -
     they'll take any drink they can!

v. pissed

sherry   olive oil   ketchup   xxxx   xxxx

Love
Tricks

wink

a poem about
↓
Spanking

Some men like their girlfriends
To be gentle, sweet and kind
But others much prefer it
If you spank their bare
behind!

a poem about
↓
Sugar Daddy Girls

Some girls like their man
to be older
It's just one of life's funny
facts
They even like bellies that
wobble around
And wrinkles and great hairy
backs!

a poem about a
Total Minger

When fixing a date up on
Facebook
Be prepared for a shock when
you meet
Your partner might look
Pretty good in their pic
But in real life might not
be so sweet!

a poem about
Protection

In case your date comes
home with you
Make sure to think ahead
Hide a pack of you-know-
whats
Right underneath your bed

my office
PRIVATE
pong
whiff